Easy Auto Sound Systems

Easy Auto Sound Systems

Use Water As Fuel!

Do you want to know RIGHT NOW how YOU can drive around using WATER AS FUEL and LAUGH at RISING GAS COSTS... while REDUCING emissions and help PREVENT GLOBAL WARMING?

While 100% "water cars" and "water trucks" are still on the drawing board, I am very excited to show you how you can start RIGHT NOW and use Water4Gas to...Convert Your Car/Truck to BURN WATER as well as Gasoline and BOOST YOUR GAS MILEAGE!!!

Easy Auto Sound Systems

Auto Sound Systems Made Easy

Contents

Duh, It's A Car Stereo! 8
How to: A Car Stereo Installation Guide 10
Pimp Up Yo' Ride! Why You Need A Good Car Stereo System 12
Ebay Has Surprising Bargains On Auto Sound Systems 14
Great Brands For Good Prices On Auto Sound Systems 16
Professional Installation Of Auto Sound Systems Imperative 18
Speakers Play the Sound but Auto Sound Systems Make It 20
The Ipod And The Auto Sound System 22
The Reasons Why You Should Add A DVD Player To Your Auto Sound System 24
XM Satellite Or Sirius For Your Auto Sound System 26
A Pioneer In Their Own Right: The Pioneer Car Stereo 28
It's A Sony Car Stereo 30
Auto Sound Systems Are Becoming Entertainment Systems 33
Choosing The Right Amplifier For Your Auto Sound System 35
Technology Spending Limits And The Auto Sound System 37
The Importance of a Good Auto Sound System 39
Is Auto Sound Systems Latest Technology A Necessity? 41

Duh, It's A Car Stereo!

If you are new to the car stereo market, you may find yourself overwhelmed at the sheer number of parts and accessories that can make up a top of the line car stereo system. In this article, we'll explore the basic components that make up a functioning car stereo system.

The Head Unit: Making It Happen

You may have seen the term "head unit" before and not known what exactly it was. Simply put the head unit is the part of your car stereo that actually produces the music from radio, tape, CD, or other device. But nowadays you can also get head units for your car stereo that can play DVDs or music and video from USB flash drives or memory cards. Head units have sure come a long ways from when people used to install home stereo equipment in their vehicles!

Amplifiers: Bring the Boom

While your head unit may provide its own internal amplification (which may be enough for you), at some point most car stereo enthusiasts will want to add amplifiers to the mix. Simply put, and amplifier takes a signal coming out of your head unit, and makes it louder. Be careful when shopping for amplifiers, as some of the large amps can draw over 100 amps; this may be well over what your alternator and battery can provide, and can cause damage to those components.

Speakers: Woofers, Tweeters, What?

The best head unit and amp is completely useless without speakers. Speakers, regardless of size, all do one thing: take the electrical signal coming from either the head unit's internal amp or your external amp and turn it into sound, usually loud sound. The different types of speakers are classified by the range of sounds they can reproduce. Tweeters, for example, only reproduce high pitches, while woofers reproduce the upper bass ranges. Midranges make midrange sounds, strangely enough, while subwoofers cover sounds from the low bass all the way down to sub sonic (those sounds you can feel but not hear). Subwoofers are usually the first candidate for external amplifiers, since they require large amounts of current to make that bone shaking bass.

Putting It All Together

Let's review: head units take your CD or tape and convert it to electrical signals. The amplifier makes this signal larger, and finally the speakers take that signal and make sound out of it. These are the base components you need for any car stereo installation. The accessories, such as crossovers and signal isolators, may or may not be needed for your particular application.

These are the basics you need to know for all car stereo systems. Now that you have a better idea what all these different terms actually mean, you should be able to shop intelligently for your new car stereo system. Just remember, as always, while you get what you pay for, you don't necessarily have to have the absolute best (and most expensive) parts for a good sound. More often than not, a midrange product will provide the best bang for your buck. And remember, it's all modular! You don't HAVE to buy every piece all at once. You can start with the head unit, and simply wire it's built in amplifier into your factory car stereo speakers. Add a sub and an amp later if you want, or replace the factory speakers with higher quality ones, it's all up to you.

How to: A Car Stereo Installation Guide

If you have ever looked into buying a new car stereo system, you probably realize that the costs of having it professionally installed can almost double the cost of your new system. But there is always the other option: do it yourself. While a car stereo installation can be complicated, there is nothing in particular that prevents you from doing it yourself, as long as you are willing to put in the time and effort to learn how before you diving into the project. Not only can you learn a lot, but there is always a sense of satisfaction when you fire it up for the first time, knowing you did it all yourself.

Patience and caution are paramount here. Some car stereo equipment is quite expensive, not to mention the price of your car to begin with! So be careful, proceed slowly, and if you have doubts, find out the answer to whatever is bothering you before you continue. Not taking it slow and carefully can lead to a botched install or even broken equipment or a damaged vehicle.

Beginners are advised to keep it simple the first time around. Don't try to install a full car theater system with LCD displays and DVD players or video games for your first installation. Start with the head unit. This is both the easiest and the most critical thing to get right the first time. Often the wiring harness that plugs into your factory stereo will need an adapter to get the correct electrical connections to the power and speaker system already in your car. And being able to reuse your factory wiring makes things much easier down the road when replacing the factory speakers. Don't just cut the harness off! Use an adapter. If you ever want to replace the head unit again, things will be much easier if you can simply unplug the old adapter and replace it with a new one for the new head unit.

The head unit will also probably require an adapter kit of some kind to fit properly in the factory dash hole. Most factory systems are either custom or what is called "Double DIN", whereas most aftermarket head units are single DIN form factor. Sometimes, filing away parts of the trim surrounding the mounting area will be needed. Do some test fits before you bolt everything down.

Speakers are a very important part of any quality audio system. While you may be able to get sound from your factory speakers with that new head unit, replacing those factory speakers with high quality aftermarket ones can make a huge difference in the quality of your sound.

For your first speaker installations, you should try to replace the speakers in the factory mounting holes. This is a fairly simple procedure, but can require removing interior panels to access the speaker mounting locations. This method is advantageous because you can use the existing brackets and wiring.

More complicated is mounting speakers in locations that didn't originally have speakers, or putting larger speakers in existing mounting locations. This will often require metalworking and building boxes and baffles to accommodate the new speakers. But if you don't have any factory speakers, or they are in bad locations, this may be your only option. Just be careful, and if the project requires a lot of reshaping of the cars metal locations, you should consider having it professionally done; this kind of work is best done with specific tools that most home enthusiasts don't have. such as plasma cutters and pneumatic sheet metal formers.

Pimp Up Yo' Ride! Why You Need A Good Car Stereo System

So you've spent thousands getting your car ready for show. New paint job, tricked out suspension, phat rims, you've got it all. But what about on the inside? A bumpin' system can be THE difference between a cool car and a truly awesome show winner.

While a killer system can make your car that much cooler, having a crap car stereo system can totally kill your cars coolness factor. This is never good if you've already spent a lot of money tricking out your vehicle. Even if you have something less than fantastically good looking, having that killer thump is guaranteed to make more people actually want to ride in your car. By the same token, a pathetic car stereo system can make your car have even less appeal than it does now.

So What Makes a Killer Car Stereo System?

Quality and attention to detail pretty much sums it up. You will never be able to get the best sound out of cheap parts, and they are more prone to failing (usually at the worst possible moment) than the more expensive parts. Little things, like the frequency of a crossover, your EQ settings, and small variations in speaker placement can make a huge difference in the overall sound of your car stereo system.

Listen around and see who has systems that sound good to you. If you can listen to several different systems in the same kind of car as yours, you will be able to get a much better idea of what sounds good and what doesn't. But even if you are listening to different car stereo systems in different vehicles than yours, you can still get a good idea of what brands of gear you like and which ones to avoid cause they sound like crap. Remember, whatever sounds the best to you in your car is the best for you! No one else can tell you what is sounds good, because listening is a very subjective experience.

Car stereo expos and conventions can be another good way of gaining listening experience, and you will usually be able to check out more different systems at one than you can find on the streets.

Auto Sound Systems Made Easy

Whatever you do, unless you have a truly awesome factory car stereo system, you will want to replace that head unit and speakers. The difference, even using factory mounting locations, can be the difference between night and day. Your mids will have more punch, your highs will be clearer and brighter, and the bass will have that bone deep thump everyone loves. Adding at least one amplified subwoofer will make a huge difference as well. You just can't get the same bass out of a 7" woofer as you can out of a 12" subwoofer.

Amplifiers are the driving force behind your car stereo system. Skimping in this area is extremely dangerous, not only to your sound quality, but to your speakers as well. An underpowered or cheaply made amplifier is prone to what is known as clipping. Without getting too technical, what this does is send a large amount of direct current through your speaker, causing the speaker coil to overheat and melt. This leads to the infamous "blown speaker". Coil overheating is the single biggest cause of speaker failure. Putting too large of an amplifier on a speaker can cause the same thing to happen. Always match up your speakers' power handling ratings to the output of your amplifier. For instance, let's say you have a 4 channel amplifier that provides 1000 watts total power. That is 250 watts per channel (1000/4), so your speakers should be capable of handling that much power, or you risk blowing them out.

Having a killer car stereo system is something your can be proud of, and dramatically increases your cars coolness factor and resale value, no matter what vehicle it is installed in.

Ebay Has Surprising Bargains On Auto Sound Systems

So you are in the market for some quality auto sound system components, or maybe an entire system, but you don't want to spend an arm and a leg on it? Ebay may be the answer to your prayers.

What is Ebay?

Anyone familiar with the internet (and many who aren't) has probably heard of Ebay. For those of you who don't know, Ebay is the worlds largest online auction house. Every day, literally thousands of auto sound system parts are auctioned off to the highest bidder, often at bargain prices significantly under normal retail cost.

Using Ebay to Find Auto Sound System Parts

Ebay can be a wonderful tool for people looking for surprisingly good bargains on auto sound system components. There are all kinds of different brands available, many of which may not be available to you locally. And these parts are often sold for less than retail. Using Ebay's search makes it easy to find the exact auto sound system parts you are looking for. Every component, from the head unit to amplifiers, speakers to accessories, and everything you need to install your auto sound system can be bought off of Ebay. You can also find installation guides, speaker boxes, sound dampening materials, and other related products there.

The Disadvantages of Ebay

There are a few things to keep in mind when bargain-hunting for auto sound system parts on Ebay. The biggest concern is that you can't listen to it before you buy it. But if you can find the same part locally, you can easily give it a test listen in their storefront. In fact, that is probably the best way to choose what parts to buy, unless you are very familiar with auto sound system components and already know exactly what you want. Then there are the general problems that come with shopping on the internet. Ebay has taken care of a lot of the problems that can come with internet shopping by implementing a rating system, wherein sellers (and buyers) are given feedback and a score based on how honestly they do business. Avoid sellers with low ratings, even if they seem to have a killer bargain. But sometimes people with no rating at all will be selling an auto sound system component. These people are first-time sellers, and can be worth a shot if you feel OK with taking a slight gamble.

Post-Purchase Installation

The last thing to keep in mind is that your new bargain auto sound system will still have to be installed. A lot of professional shops give a discount to the installation or the parts when you purchase and install in one location. Sometimes, this can wind up being cheaper than buying off of Ebay and having your local shop install the system at their full rates. But if you feel confident that you can do it, you can always attempt the installation on your own. This will save you a LOT of money, but if your system is particularly complex, you may wish to have it done professionally. While more expensive up front, this could save you a lot of time and maybe even money if you crack that shiny new LCD panel trying to fit it yourself.

Great Brands For Good Prices On Auto Sound Systems

So you want to juice up that pathetic factory sound system, but the price of some auto sound system equipment is making your wallet shiver in fear? Don't worry, with a little bit of smart shopping you can put together a system that will blow your factory sound away, without spending your entire savings to do it.

Online Shopping

If you are willing and able to install the system yourself, and have listened to a bunch of systems and gotten an idea of the brands of auto sound system parts you want, you can find great deals shopping for your parts online. Even if you don't want to do the installation yourself, the Internet is still a great place to shop for the best deals on name brand equipment.

Shopping Locally

Again, if you are willing to do the installation yourself, or are looking to upgrade your existing system, you can find good deals locally a lot of the time. Even though auto sound system shops often have higher prices than online stores, a good bit of the price of any auto sound system is the installation. You can often get away with paying retail if you do the install yourself, and get a great deal on a killer sound system in the process. The main advantage to shopping locally is that you can listen to the different systems before you buy, which is just not possible when shopping on the Internet.

Hit the Pawn Shops

If you both have a good idea of the brands of auto sound system equipment you want and are willing to purchase used equipment, you can shop around your local pawn shops. You can find some really bargain-basement prices in these shops, and usually any gear that a pawn shop buys is tested and working. All auto sound system components, from head units to speakers and amplifiers, are available at pawn shops all over.

The best total prices are still only obtainable by installing the system yourself; if you are not confident in your abilities, it can still be worth it have even used parts professionally installed since it can be much easier to put different parts in once the wiring and brackets are all in place, making it more of a plug and play operation.

Name Brands at Good Prices

While everyone would like to have top of the line JL Audio competition speakers or the like, the prices on the very best auto sound system components can be astronomical. You can easily spend over $500 on a single speaker at the very top end. But there are plenty of quality midrange products from companies like Kenwood, Alpine, and JVC. Stay away from the absolute bottom of the barrel parts, though, as they can often sound worse than your existing factory system You do not want to spend a bunch of money only to have it sound the same or worse than your existing system. The midrange products are usually the way to go for the best price vs. performance. And with some careful product selection and shopping, you can build a kicking system for under $400 if you do the installation yourself.

Professional Installation Of Auto Sound Systems Imperative

So you just dropped $800 for a good auto sound system. Now comes one of the hardest decisions you will have to make: do I get this system installed professionally or do it myself? While you may be very tempted to do it yourself and avoid spending another $300 or more having it professionally installed, you need to ask yourself several questions before you decide to do it yourself.

Can I Do This Myself?

The first question you need to ask yourself and answer honestly is "Can I really do this on my own?". Installing an auto sound system is no easy task. It requires concentration, a certain proficiency at mechanical tasks, and a fair amount of specialized knowledge. Something as simple as running too small a wire can cause physical damage to your expensive components, and some of the more common problems like ground loop noise or alternator whine can be difficult to fix if you don't know the electrical theory behind it all. Mounting speakers and your head unit usually requires some sort of modifications to your cars body and dash, and if not done properly can damage your vehicle and look lousy. Even installing a subwoofer requires enough knowledge of acoustics and how sound actually propagates to be able to build an enclosure that sounds good and works with your subwoofer rather than against it.

If none of the preceding examples made much sense to you, then you are probably better off having your auto sound system professionally installed. It will save you a lot of time, headache, and quite possibly money of you damage expensive components or your vehicle.

But if you have some idea what all this means, or are willing to spend a couple of weeks learning all the ins and outs involved, then doing it yourself may be a viable option.

Do I Want To Do This Myself?

Even if you either already are capable enough, or feel confident you could learn how well enough to do it yourself, you may not want to. For one thing, doing a good job of installing even the most basic auto sound system takes a lot of time and effort spent cramped in your cars interior. Wires, screws, and other things you have to get at invariably seem to be in the most awkward locations. In some cars, even getting the part of the dash off you will need to can be a nightmare. Having a professional do it can save you a lot of time and effort, and will usually wind up with you listening to the system you just dropped big bucks on a lot sooner. Plus, any shop worth going to will offer a warranty on their work. So if some wiring they install shorts out in the future, you may be covered for any damage resulting from it. This can be especially important in auto sound systems, since they are routinely subjected to vibration, shock, dust, and temperature extremes.

Sound Quality is Paramount

If you think that installing an auto sound system is as simple as hooking everything up and going off down the road, you probably don't need to be doing the installation yourself. After hooking everything up comes probably the hardest part to get right for the amateur: tuning the new system. Things like crossover frequencies, overall sound balance, and the precise speaker locations can make a HUGE difference in the way your system sounds at the end. If you don't know exactly what to listen for, and don't have some audio tuning CDs, your sound will be very suboptimal. Even though it may sound alright to you, you will be amazed at how much better a properly tuned auto sound system can sound. A professional can more than likely do a much better job of this in less time than you can.

Speakers Play the Sound but Auto Sound Systems Make It

When building or upgrading an auto sound system, the first thing most people look into are the speakers. While speakers do play a very large role in the overall sound of your system, there are many other things that must be taken into consideration if you are going to avoid "over-speakering". It's not necessary with modern technology and enclosures to take your entire trunk up with giant subwoofers to get that bone shakin bass you want.

The Head Unit

Good sound starts at the source. And in the case of auto sound systems, this source is the head unit. This is the CD player in your dash that actually provides the signals that the rest of your system amplifies and plays back. You can have the best speakers and amps in the world, but if you pair that with a cheap head unit with a lousy DAC, your sound will be lousy. In fact, with good speakers and amps, any shortcomings in your head unit will become glaringly obvious; the speakers will faithfully reproduce everything fed to them, including the hiss caused by a cheap DAC and op amps.

The Amplifiers

Again, the best way to get killer sound is to start at the source and work your way to the output. After you have a good quality head unit that makes a clean audio signal, you need quality amplifiers to take this signal and push it still clean to your speakers. Cheap amps will often introduce noise into your signal, whether through lousy signal to noise ratios, or ground loop/alternator whine caused by poor internal or external grounds. Again, with good, speakers, any problems with your amplifiers will be very audible as your killer speakers faithfully reproduce every bit of the signal the amps provide - including any noise.

The Speakers

And finally, you should consider the speakers themselves. The biggest two things to remember are quality makes a huge difference, and bigger is not always better. If you listen to a lot of music with extremely fast bass hits, like techno, using 15" subwoofers will make your bass line muddy and indistinct. For this type of music, 10" or 12" is the largest subwoofer you want to push. If you listen to rap or other music with extremely low frequency and rhythmic bass hits, a 15" may be what you want. In all cases, mounting the speakers in a properly tuned bandpass enclosure will ensure the best quality sound.

The Speaker Enclosure

The sound you get out of the exact same speaker/amp combination will be very different depending on the enclosure you put it in. A simple sealed enclosure will provide a fairly neutral, flat response across the frequency curve of your speaker. A properly tuned bandpass enclosure can either help make up for a deficient area in your response curve, or amplify the frequencies you really want to add punch to.

While speakers are often the first thing considered when building an auto sound system, they really should be near the last on your list. Only after you have a quality head unit and amplifiers to drive them should you worry about your speakers. Even moving your current speakers into different types of enclosures can make an enormous difference in your sound quality.

The Ipod And The Auto Sound System

Apple Computer, maker of the iPod, has a cultural phenomenon on their hands. The iPod is the single most popular personal music listening device on the market today. Its ability to store large amounts of music, coupled with its tiny size and ease of use, has made it a hit across all age groups. Not even PC giant Microsoft's competing Zune has even put a dent into iPod sales. And the market for iPod accessories has grown along with it's popularity.

What does all this have to do with auto sound systems, you ask? Well, since the iPod is such a popular product, it was perhaps inevitable that auto sound system manufacturers would begin adding the ability to interface your head unit with your iPod. It just makes too much sense, both from a business and a usability standpoint. There are a quite a few products aimed specifically at integrating the iPod with your vehicles sound system. Heading the pack are head units that allow the iPod to be plugged directly into the head unit face. These types of units allow the user to control their iPod through the standard interface, often displaying all the meta-info that is included, such as song title, artist, album, length, bitrate, et cetera.

If your head unit already has a USB port, you are good to go as well. There are adapters to allow your iPod to act as any other USB music storage device while connected to your auto sound system. Playback can either be controlled from the head unit itself, or through the iPod, depending on your specific system and the adapter used.

If your head unit doesn't have either of these ports, don't despair. Most aftermarket head units will have line level inputs on the back, or a jack for an external cd player input (this jack often looks just like a headphone jack) that can be used with a special cradle for your iPod to allow you to playback through your auto sound system. These types of systems require you to select the song you want on your iPod directly; they simply provide a line-level output of whatever you are playing at the moment on the iPod.

All of the above systems can provide power to your iPod as well, both charging its internal batteries and keeping it running for as long as you care to listen.

Auto Sound Systems Made Easy

If you are shopping around for a new auto sound system, adds are you either own an iPod or have thought about getting one. Keep an eye out for iPod interface features when looking for a new head unit. Even if you don't have an iPod now, it is better to be able to simply buy one and plug it in later than to have to replace your head unit or settle for a suboptimal way of handling your iPod playback control. If you think there is any chance you will have an iPod in the future, you should seriously consider getting a head unit compatible with it now, and save the hassle in the future. When you get your iPod, you will have the ultimate in portable music playback system ready to go for your listening enjoyment.

The Reasons Why You Should Add A DVD Player To Your Auto Sound System

Whether you are in the market for your first auto sound system, or are looking for the next upgrade to your already great one, you should consider getting a head unit with integrated DVD playback. These come in a few different varieties to fit different budgets and desires. Read on to find out more about these bits of ultra-cool tech.

Integrated Display Head Units

There are head units available that have integrated LCD panels to display both DVD video and information or cool visualizations during audio playback. Some of these integrated panels are even touch sensitive, allowing total control of your player via the video display. The panels may either be fixed and visible at all times, or have motorized slide-out action that keeps the display hidden when not in use.

The major advantage of these types of units is they are pretty much plug and play. There is no need for the additional expense of both an external panel and the installation of it. You pay for this ease of installation and lower cost by having a (usually) much smaller display than buying one separately.

Video-Capable Head Units

These types of head units usually have an integrated DVD player, but display the video on separate LCD panels hooked up to a video output on the back of the unit. These units are somewhat cheaper than the ones with integrated displays (especially the touchscreen versions), but have the additional expense of a separate LCD panel that must be purchased and installed. You can get much larger panels than are available on the all in one units, and can select the ones that best fit your budget and viewing preferences. Plus, these kinds of head units can drive multiple displays for the ultimate in awesomeness.

Hybrid Head Units

Auto Sound Systems Made Easy

These types of head units have both an integrated video panel which may or may not be touch sensitive, and also provide external video outputs. These kinds of head units are the most expensive, but provide lots of flexibility in installation, display options, and control. You can easily add additional panels later on, using the integrated display in the meantime. I recommend this type of video head unit over both of the others, as it is both usable out of the box and provides the most future-proofing of all three choices in terms of expansion capabilities.

Regardless of which type you choose to use, it is highly recommended that you have these installed by professionals. Mounting an LCD panel in a car and making it look good, be functional, and safe is a job best left to a professional. LCD panels are extremely easy to crack if you aren't careful installing them, and since a car is a vibration prone environment, they must be mounted as securely as possible to avoid breaking later. And they are not cheap! Anytime you are dealing with such expensive equipment, it is best to have the installation handled by professionals who can provide a warranty. And a lot of manufacturers won't warranty your parts unless you do have them installed by a professional shop. If you are going to spend the money on a video head unit for your auto sound system, you should spend the extra to make sure that it is installed right the first time.

XM Satellite Or Sirius For Your Auto Sound System

It took approximately 18 months longer than anticipated to bring satellite radio to the general public. That's not so bad, actually, considering the complexity of the technology involved. The latest contribution to consumer entertainment has generated significant attention, and as XM and Sirius become more readily available and agreeable to consumers, chances are good they will have a healthy future. So far, XM is leading the charge with more than two million subscribers to Sirius' roughly half million. Although, unlike the VCR issue, it would appear there won't be one winner and one loser. Both satellite systems are strong, have incredible programming and talented personnel, on the air and behind the scenes, and possess ambitious and, most importantly, attainable business strategies.

The strength and longevity to each service's ongoing success are through their multiple automotive alliances. XM is partially owned by General Motors, and its subsidiary, Hughes Electronics. On the other side of the table, Daimler has invested a significant sum of money in Sirius. Both companies count on exclusive partnerships with these OEMs and other retailers to carry their hardware and offer their programming packages to buyers of their partners'/investors' vehicles. In addition to the Mercedes model and the Chrysler Group lines, Sirius enjoys an exclusive relationship with BMW and MINI and also a strong relationship with the Ford family, including its P A G. Both programmers share Porsche, Nissan and Infiniti and other vehicle models.

For XM, the affiliation with GM is an extremely important one, as the auto manufacturer has pursued an aggressive marketing push to attract customers who will purchase XM-equipped vehicles and ultimately become subscribers. The bottom line is that these impressive content developers are performing what many motorists would consider a community service: providing multiple musical choices and allowing consumers to shut off conventional, mainstream broadcast radio stations filled with mindless commercials, limited play lists and ceaselessly irritating talk shows.

XM offers 68+ channels of commercial-free music programming, along with 33 news, sports and talk show stations, plus 21 dedicated traffic and weather channels, and Sirius featuring roughly the same total number of channels, 120, with 65 commercial-free, including constant traffic and

Auto Sound Systems Made Easy

weather reports in the top 20 U.S. markets. These leaves a consumer spoilt for choice. Fortunately, both services offer their proprietary hardware through a number of retail chains enabling the user to easily subscribe, in order to receive all the music, talk and sports that basic AM/FM formats can't.

Sirius' offers "plug and play" marketing strategy. This allows a consumer to take the portable-styled unit from the car into the home and connect the unit to his or her stereo receiver. XM on it's side offers a similar strategy, securing many of the leading audio manufacturers to produce XM-ready radios that can replace existing head units in a customer's vehicle, as well as the Delphi XM Roady, which includes an XM receiver, micro-antenna and cassette adaptor available for the car or truck in one small package.

There are multiple subscription packages available, and consumers can sign-up for the appropriate service through their dealership and even roll the service's fee into their monthly car payment. Retail chains such as Circuit City and Best Buy also enable consumers to sign up on-site for one or the other service. XM offers its programming package for $9.95 per month, while Sirius is a bit more expensive at $12.95. However, Sirius gets quite creative with a series of payment structures, offering a number of free months based on the length of a customer's contract. For a fee of $499.00, a consumer can have Sirius for "the lifetime of the product." Even Hertz has joined the ranks, offering Sirius in 30,000 rental cars across the country for a nominal daily fee.

Whichever system you prefer, both sound like a good deal. With the depth of material both satellite services present, singing along with Janet Jackson's, Linking Park or Elton just got pretty easier. But remember that even with the above options present, it won't eliminate the need for a new auto sound system, though the type of auto sound system may pose some cretain requirements.

A Pioneer In Their Own Right: The Pioneer Car Stereo

If you have ever taken a ride in some posh car, whether a friends or associates or even driven one yourself, then you are probably familiar with the super fine and cool music that is the reserve of such vehicles, ever wondered where that sizzling jazz or hypnotic ballad is coming from? Look no further than the dashboard, where you are sure to find an unmistakable cool Pioneer Auto Stereo unit plugged up into the dashboard console with super speakers to boot, and an array of accessories like Pioneer navigational devices, and Pioneer LCD panels. Maybe this is one reason as to why Pioneer Car Stereo/products have commanded such a massive support the world over.

Based in Tokyo Japan, the Pioneer Corporation is undoubtedly a world champion in leading digital consumer entertainment products. Pioneer was founded in 1938 as a Tokyo based small scale speaker and radio repair store, and has immensely grown to be world-renowned leader in consumer electronics industry and Pioneer Car Stereo affirms that.

The Pioneer corporation truly deserves of it's name. Among their many wonder innovations are products like the well known interactive cable TV, Pioneer Compact disc player for car, the Laser powered Disc player, not to forget the very first Pioneer removable face Car Stereo, Systems for DVD recording , organic electroluminescent display, and plasma display. Their technology mastery in display and optical disc products is well complemented by it's first class software products and unbeatable manufacturing ability.

Pioneer branded Car Stereo units have moved away from just plain and simple head units, and now a typical car stereo is easily composed of numerous elements built into the car console. Tangible items like DVD player with LCD panels, navigational devices, together with an array of standard items like compact discs, cassette and mp3 players are now consolidated and compatible. It would be a little disappointment not to acquire this devices, as it is true pleasure to see them all work in harmony. Traditionally, a Pioneer Stereo is made up of a head set together with a cassette, radio, or cd player. However common place this may sound, anybody is surely bound to be astonished with the excellent quality sound and superb features that Pioneer Car Stereo offers.

Auto Sound Systems Made Easy

The PioneerAuto Stereo DEH-P90HDD solo CD player head set lets you record audio for CD (from a changer or the unit itself) onto a 10GB or more hard disk drive, which has a content capacity of almost 200 audio CD's (that use ATRAC3 digital compression). These CDs are well identified by the already installed Gracenote CDDB database, this incorporates self-play lists that make searching of specific CDs fast and simple. This wonder Pioneer Car Stereo system unit will play your MP3 CD's plus audio CDs, CD-R and CD-RW discs too. Its MagicGate Memory stick player will also allow you to play recorded Memory stick audio files with ease. The incorporated organic EL display is simple to read and allows image downloads; this makes its look customizable. The In-built DSP provides a 13-band graphic EQ and a large range of tools. The Pioneer DEH-P90HDD comes XM ready and is equipped with a steering wheel remote.

If you fancy cassettes, then the KEH-P4020 model of Pioneer Car Stereo for cassette player with a head unit is probably good product for you. It's a fully logic cassette with multi-colored display panel, EEQ™ equalizer system, 45Wx4 High Power, IP-Bus System Control, Tuner, flap face and has an easily removable face security. So, if you are contemplating to purchase a Pioneer Car Stereo unit, it would be wise to suite it with good Pioneer speakers, these too bring together technological success of Pioneer IASCA award winning Premier Reference Series (PRS) speakers, these REV series of speakers boasts of Pioneer's Kevlar Fiber Composite Cones, Wave guides and Soft-dome tweeters. Every speaker comes equipped with a dazzling yellow cone and noticeable wave-guides, and a six-spoke grill coated with titanium finish that bears chrome wheels look.

I guess, these marvelous products are the main reason as to why the Pioneer auto Car Stereo is branded Pioneer, they are truly unbeatable.

It's A Sony Car Stereo

Sony is big, command respect, and of course you bet, well represented and respected. With its brand name Ubiquitous, Sony slogan is in every electronic consumers lips. The Sony made brands range from the -Aibo, you guessed right!! To the play station and the Vaio. Sony is a power innovator who have excelled in almost every consumer electronic under the sky.

The Tokyo based Sony Corporation, is a world leader in the manufacture of video, audio, information technology and communications products both for professional and consumer markets. Speak of Sony in motion picture, Sony in music, Sony in computer entertainment, and even Sony in E-commerce, all of which shape the comprehensive list of entertainment companies that make Sony such a giant to reckon in the world.

No wonder, it isn't astonishing to discover that Sony Car Stereo is a well known product in the auto audio market. Sony introduced their newest carrier car stereos audio product in 1995, the Sony Auto Stereo from the Xplod family series comes equipped with subwoofers, amplifiers, CD changers and other accessories making it extraordinary, in both functionality and aesthetic values.

The best head set unit in the Sony Xplod family series of Car Stereo is unmistakably the CDX - M9900 CD changer/ Receiver and Controller with MP3 Player, which comes equipped with the features below:

- Power Compliant CEA-2006.
- External Source Playback Video Input.
- 4-voltage F/R/Sub Pre-outs w/HPF & LPF
- 32,000+ colored TFT display
- High Power (52W x 4)
- CD Text ,CD/MD Control,.
- D/A Converter(1-bit)
- 120db S/N Ratio (Drive-S).
- (XM Ready).
- EQ7,BBE MP, DSO.
- (Auxiliary Input parts)

Auto Sound Systems Made Easy

- 18FM+ & 12AM presets with SSIR-EXA tuner,
- (Plus Red Key illumination)
- Wireless rotary remote (RM-X6s)- optional.
- Wired rotary remote (RM-X45s)- Optional
- Provided wireless remote card (RM-X145A)

This Sony Auto Stereo works even better when installed with the following complement items from the same Xplod family series:

Sony Car stereo Model XS - V6941H with "6 x 9" - way speakers.

- Surround Stroke stabilizer
- Cone Mid "2-5/8"
- Cone Mid "6 x 9"
- (100W RMS) 400W Peak Power
- Durable and adaptable set up Options

Sony Car Stereo with XS-L102P5 10" Subwoofer:

- Polypropylene Cone-10"
- (330W RMS) 1200W Peak Power
- Special cone design provides exceptional rigidity
- Binding Posts gold-plated
- Optimized Small sealed/band pass enclosure.
- Voice Coil (4-Ohm)
- Subwoofer Parameters -2005

Sony Car Stereo with XM-2100GTX 2/1 able Channel Amplifier:

- Max Power "600W"
- 20Hz-20kHz @ 0.04% THD 100W x 2 RMS to 4 ohms,
- 20Hz-20kHz at 0.1% THD 250W times 1 RMS into 4 ohms,

© Wings Of Success

- Power Compliant (CEA-2006)
- "Variable 50 to 300 Hz lower filter pass
- 40+ Hz EQ booster.
- MOSFET power supply
- Speaker level inputs & RCA.

Similar to most audio carmakers, this Sony Car Stereo also gives you some video playing compatible units like DVDs and VCDs. Another extra dream system from the Sony Stereo for Car series is undoubtedly the **MV- 900sds portable DVD Dream System unit.**

- In-built Stereo Speakers
- AV Input/Output.
- Dolby Digital®, & dts®) Optical Digital Output
- Wireless headphones IR transmitter
- Wireless headphone- 2 sets included.
- Remote wireless card included.
- In-built wired FM modulator
- Display image, reversible.
- Slot-load capable DVD Mechanism
- Branded Memory Stick® media for JPEG, MPEG, MP3 playback.
- TFT display 9" wide screen with swivel function
- /CD-R/ DVD/RW/VCD/ & MP3 Playback feature.

The encasement for this amazing unit has a metallic grey finish, ideally attached to the vehicle ceiling.

It is also worth noting that many enthusiasts incorporate the Sony play station with their Sony Stereos for Car, something that may explain why Sony Automotive Stereo system has developed quite a following.

Auto Sound Systems Are Becoming Entertainment Systems

We all like shopping, and window shopping in particular is even more fun. But what if you have been doing some real shopping, for example, shopping for an Auto Sound System. It's most likely that you've come across a myriad of Auto Audio Systems and Entertainment Systems and many more while treating yourself to a shopping spree. Auto Audio System makers are these days going to the extreme to offer you everything from headphones (perhaps adjustable), individual speakers to headphones, and what about dual players that can allow different audio formats to be played in one sector of the car than another. Marvel of technology perhaps. All this brilliant and convenient devices and much more are aimed at enticing and luring you the consumer to spent more of your cash on these fancy designed Auto Sound System. Be it an MP3 that directly connects to the Auto Audio systems of your car or truck, you will find it.

It remains and will always be a security concern, especially for the safety Conscious among us, about the justification of having a DVD System in your vehicle. Notwithstanding that, a majority of the populace will continue to equip their automobiles with DVD players for sound and entertainment. Auto Audio System manufacturers on their side will continue to improve and beautifully package these devices while offering extraordinary offers on installation. This of course goes contrary to popular believe that all this offers distraction to drivers. I belong to a group of the few who feel that in these technology driven days of PDAs, Notebooks, Fast Foods, Instant coffee, and multitasking, a DVD or VCD at the back is one of the ideal element that can be added to a vehicle to provide that much needed distraction at times from daily road rage and hassles of daily commute.

Though I'm not surprised that many people don't seem to see what this is got to do with an Audio Sound System, somehow I understand them. One of the magical features being offered by Auto Audio System product manufacturers is an aspect that permits back seated passengers to use individual headphones together with mini LCD screens build into the head rests to see and hear what is being played by the DVD system player in the front without causing distraction to the driver.

It's an understandable fact that having noise from a back placed DVD player is akin to the distraction caused by the presence of disgruntled preteens fighting for your attention from their

Auto Sound Systems Made Easy

seats in the back or listening to audio books while commandeering the vehicle altogether. I without shame confess that audio books are one of my readily admitted addictions. I mostly limit my books to interesting and well-liked stories that are suited for children whenever I'm riding with kids along, because it mostly saves the steamy and sometimes riotous account of Stephanie Plum for when I'm driving alone. Another good reason is to have an Auto Audio System that both reads and understands MP3.

This technology is a reality and available and We should expect to see more amazing innovations that speak technologically of Auto Systems for Sound and entertainment in the future. Our world is technologically active and evolutions spanned by innovations are inevitable. This makes the possibility of wonderful features a realizable reality in the near future.

Whether you are a newbie to modern technology or its your biggest nemesis, or just enjoy riding its wave, it won't stop down. This sounds the alarm that the days of old and its obsolete products including Auto Sounds Systems are fast coming to an end. Hence the comic yarn that we are swiftly being converted into a society that's edging up towards the "Jetson's envisioned future" I therefore bemoan my deficiency of a Rosie. At most I'm joy filled to see that novel technologies in Auto Sound Systems are indeed versatile to offering more than before.

Auto Sound Systems Made Easy

Choosing The Right Amplifier For Your Auto Sound System

Setting about to find the best Amplifier for your sound system could be a whole lot simpler if you just dedicate sometime before hand to learn what is best for you and will perform best with your type of car, truck or SUV's audio system. It's worthwhile to learn about the functions of an Amplifier for you to make an informed purchase; the major function of an Amplifier is that is receives small sound signal from your auto sound system and increases it to produce louder sound. This means that the more powerful your Amplifier, the more exceptional quality sound it produces. A lesser-powered Amplifier will therefore have a weak, thin sound that is quite unappealing in any auto sound system and most other sound system as well.

It is also worth mentioning that power rating of an Amplifier is determined by the utmost power it's able to expend and not by it's regular usage amount. RMS rating is a good indicator of an Amplifier power output. Another thing to consider is that never purchase an Amplifier based only on RMS rating or maximum output. This number can be remarkably misleading in Amplifier purchse.If your preference is towards a thumping driving bass beat, then ensure that your Amplifier is equipped with a bass boost button. Such a button will be a plus in giving you a bass boost. I sure believe this is a must have to most bass lovers. Not every Amplifier is equipped with this, so shop smart in accordance to your likes.

Amplifiers are essentially divided into four main classes (but of course, there are many more classes, though mostly uncommon, so I will not dwell much on defining them) which represent excellent quality you ought to expect from the system.

A) 1. This is a class with amazing production of superior sound, but the down side is that it wastes large amount of energy in producing that good quality sound.
B) 2. This class is somewhat better than 1 as far as energy consumption is concerned, but it is a bit worse as it produces lesser quality sound.
C) 1/2. This is like a cross-breed between 1 and 2 because energy and sound wastage depends on the volume. Low volumes will use the class 1 attribute of the Amplifier while higher volumes are more in maintaining with class 2.
D) 3. This is mostly decent in producing good quality bass sound and nothing more. The quantity of sound and energy wastage is both moderate and is neither very impressive.

Auto Sound Systems Made Easy

This is of course a skeleton run through most of the core amplifier basics. It is also worth noting that a score of people these days talk of amplifiers as just Amps, instead of fully pronouncing the entire word Am-pl-i-fi-er, maybe it's too long for most folks or just a hype. It's probably a slang widely accepted that no one would blink an eye if you utter it. Infact if you go the so-called old way and call it AMPLIFIER, don't be surprised if you get funny looks. Despite of all these, Amplifiers aren't the end to all that would be of an automobile sound system. its necessity is determined by you the consumer, because as a matter of fact most audio sound system work well, minus the extras like an amplifier that only serves to justify the price raise.

A decision to buy an Amplifier for your latest auto sound system, truck or SUV is at one moment filled with excitement and exhilaration, because this is habitually a decision that you have introspected over time. This same excitement can result to fear at later stage, due to the absence of clarity in what you truly need. I presume that this has at least gone a distance in informing your decision on whether or not to purchase an Amplifier, and if your answer happens to fall in the affirmative, you will ultimately make an informed decision prior to purchase.

Technology Spending Limits And The Auto Sound System

Ours is a world where technology has become a necessary and regular companion. We take it with us to the beach, we find it at the work place, in the gymnasium, and even our leisure and communication needs are dominated by it. It only makes sense that in our cars we would like to have the best technologically possible auto sound systems our hard earned money can buy. The problem is that new technology especially in auto sound systems is being introduced to the market each and every day at unfathomable rate and many of us feel as though if we hold our breath just a little bit longer something even superior and more impressive will come along. We know that we will absolutely want to kick ourselves if we buy in to "that or this" company's auto sound system that was exceptional yesterday, just before the next great thing hits the market.

The fact remains that advanced auto sound system technology is already here with us and the question isn't if it will hit the market but rather when. And when seems to be a pretty big question when it comes to emerging technologies. There are always so many things that control when the actual product will hit the shelves in stores or even how much supply will be available at that point in time. The really good news for consumers is that if you wait until that point, chances are the prices on the system you like now will probably lower significantly almost overnight.

While the tech-savvy in me would love to have the hottest and greatest of gadgetry at all times, the dad in me knows that the kids will need braces, new shoes for soccer, and (ultimately) tuition for college. For those reasons, I will continue using my sadly old-fashioned electronic Machine and secretly long for the brand new notebook while listening to the latest tunes on my iPod Shuffle while secretly longing for one of the new iPods, which is capable of playing video. I will live however, and will enjoy watching others play with their new gadgetary goodies while I learn about them and wait for the prices to drop (just like DVD players a few years back).

I can declare myself at least smart enough to understand that most of the time it is best not to be the first to buy a new product or an emerging technology. Let someone else take the risks associated with buying an essentially untried product while I sit back and listen to what they have to say. This way I can make an informed decision without bearing the scars associated with testing an untried product.

Auto Sound Systems Made Easy

There are many things I'm willing to sacrifice and many more things I give to my children as test objects. The thing I have discovered quite often with them is that if it can survive a few weeks in their care, it is a pretty safe bet and might even be worth purchasing stock in the company. We all have some things that are more important to us than others and while I love technology there are other things I love more including fancy auto sound systems.

Music, however, is a very important part of my life and I do try to keep current with the latest and greatest when it comes to auto sound systems. My favorite at the moment is the Pioneer car stereo. Every piece of this equipment is designed with the idea of making music sound, as it should. You can get the biggest and greatest sound quality from this auto sound system without giving up half your trunk or your entire back seat. Pioneer is one of the more expensive products on the market when it comes to auto sound systems but it is well worth every dime.

While considering your options for an auto sound system be sure to keep in mind that the most expensive product is not necessarily the best product-no matter what the salesman tells you. By learning as much as possible about all choices you may find that one of the less expensive systems is actually better suited for your auto sound system needs. In so doing you wil probably spent many blissful nights knowing that the auto sound system you purchased is the best investment for your money.

The Importance of a Good Auto Sound System

You might be a great fun of David Letterman, and if you are, then I'm sure you've seen and heard his crazy and often hilarious top 10 lists. He has become famous for them and they have been often imitated but never quite aptly duplicated by many around the world. Though I have no intentions of trying to claim or even hope to be as funny as Letterman is, I would love to create a top 5 list of why you need a new auto sound system. The sad part is that some of this may ring true for many, but if not, I bet it will at least put a smile on your face.

-The reason number one of why you should get a new auto sound system is that the 8-trac went out of fashion long before your first child was born. Even though you've clung to the past, it has finally met its limitations of usefulness and it is time to move along and embrace the wonderful world of modern technology and what it can mean to you and the time you and your family spend riding in your automobile. And this probably means getting a good quality Auto Sound System that will indeed add value and beauty to your commuting time.

-The second reason, though somewhat funny might be to compete with your Aunt Deborahl who has cataracts and also owns a better auto sound system than you. Believe me I know this one stings a little, especially when it hits home. We all hate to think that someone that is older has a more technologically hip and sound auto product than we do. We often like to kid ourselves into thinking that we live on the cutting edge of technology when that is probably far from the case. Aunt Deborah probably has the kicking auto sound system she does so that it can be heard without the assistance of miracle ear so keep that in mind before you pull all of your hair out.

- The third reason might stem from the fact that, because you're tired of your auto audio system crummy speakers that seem to play static more often than music and make more popping and snapping sounds than your old fashioned popcorn popper. Speakers are often only a small part of how your auto sound system runs. Chances are if you are currently having speaker problems, an entirely new auto sound system is going to be an ideal option in ensuring that all your problems are fixed and solved to your complete satisfaction.

- The fourth one might be as a result of your Amazon odyssey that brought you to a Weird Al Yankovich you just can't seem to refuse when it comes to last minute bargains in the world's largest garage sale. The truth of the matter is that Amazon can be an excellent resource as far as auto sound systems go. It is important however, to remember that you really need to hear the system before you spend your hard earned money buying it and a lot of time and/or money on the installation of the auto sound system you select. For that reasonAmazon may not be the best choice for your particular needs.

- Finally, maybe you really hate your neighbors and secretly hope that a loud enough, late night thumping from your cars auto sound system will convince them to move. Admittedly not the kindest of reasons for the need of a new auto sound system but if you've had some of my previous neighbors I am fairly certain that it isn't too bad of an idea. Just be careful not to shake too much or they may be leaving part of their automobiles behind.

Don't forget that modern auto sound systems are loaded with amazing features; ranging from XML programming, an endless array of subscription programs, and many more. All of which combine to give you a superb commuting experience. But that doesn't change the fact that the true and real importance of a good auto sound system lies not in their attached price tag, its minute details of manufacturing, or even the bass they flaunt. True beauty of an auto sound system will always be in the quality of sound it provides which must be music and not noise to your ears.

Is Auto Sound Systems Latest Technology A Necessity?

Music is a darling the world over , if not just a frequent companion in our daily lives. It accompanies us to the beach, to the workplace, equally on our numerous bike rides or phone conversations. Isn't it of good judgment that we fancy to equip our SUVs, Sedans, or whatever you drive, with possibly the best auto sound systems you can lay your hands on. The drawback is that novel technology is making it to the markets at a rapid rate than we can possibly keep up with, be it on daily or monthly basis, its happening fast. No wonder we are absolutely quick to kick ourselves in the butt when deciding whether to buy this or maybe that company's made auto sound system. We are truly spoiled for choice.

Matter-of-factly, excellent technology in auto sound system already exists. The question therefore isn't whether or not it will reach the market, but instead when. When? hence becomes a really a considerable question in discussing about new technologies. There are numerous factors that control the duration it takes for an actual product to reach the market and the supply availability at the point in time. Good news is that consumers are a patient lot, and will always wait until that point approaches; it then pays to realize that prices for these systems you love will drop almost overnight.

Though I may prefer to procure one of these star gadgets like everyone else does, I have to remind myself of my obligations as a parent, which are to ensure that my children are well fed, clothed and educated, College fees don't come easy remember. This reasons will therefore keep me hooked to my old-fashioned machine while deep down longing for the newest Acer notebooks, I'll play my tracks on my Ipod Shuffle while longing for a new Ipods that can play video. Life will however go on, and I will enjoy playing spectator to those playing with their new fancy gadgets, while also learning from them and waiting for prices to go down. (Just like Mp3s a few years ago).

I can consider myself smart enough for realizing that it's mostly not wise to be the first buyer of new products or new technology. Better let someone take the expensive risk associated with purchasing untested product and get their first hand opinion of the product. This will go miles in informing your decisions minus the risks that come with new untested products.

Auto Sound Systems Made Easy

There are countless things I can sacrifice and many others I'm willing to go the extra mile in order to give my children as test objects. What I have come to realize is that if the item or device can survive for weeks under their care, it is a good bet and is without doubt worth buying stock in the company. Most of us have things we consider most important than others and though I love technology, there are other things of higher priority.

I treasure music, and it's a very important part of my life, I therefore try my best to keep up with the best and latest when choosing auto sound systems. My most preferred happens to be the Bose. This system is wholly designed to make music sound as it ought to. You can find the best quality and greatest audio from this system without sacrificing half your trunk or the whole back seat. Bose is an expensive product on the market when it comes to auto sound systems, but all the same worth your money.

Always remember that the best auto sound system is not necessarily the most expensive auto sound product in the market, this is good piece of advice when considering your options in regard to auto sound system, this stands true, regardless of what the salesman tells you. Learning all that you possibly can, about the choices available in auto sound system, might make you discover that there are less costlier systems well suited to your auto sound system than you previously thought.

This Product Is Brought To You By